# See Gail.

# Gail likes to paint.

Gail likes to paint with
her paint pail.

# See Kate and Jake by the lake with the cake?

4

Oh, no! Green paint!

# Gail and her paint pail!

# See the green seed?

Oh, no! Blue paint!

Gail and her paint pail!

# See five mice who like the ice?

10

# Oh, no! Gold paint!
# Gail and her paint pail!

# See the old, gold boat and the goat?

Oh, no! More blue paint!
Gail and her paint pail!

See Duke the blue mule?

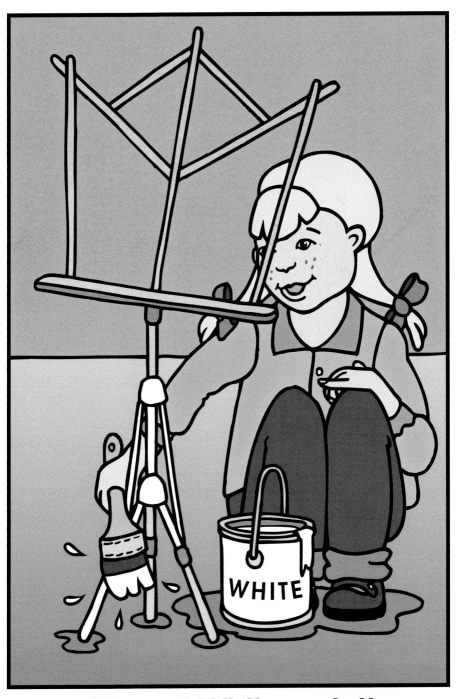

# Oh, no! White paint!
# Gail and her paint pail!

# Gail likes to paint with her paint pail!